Editor
Eric Migliaccio

Managing Editor
Ina Massler Levin, M.A.

Editor-in-Chief
Sharon Coan, M.S. Ed.

Illustrator
Bruce Hedges

Cover Artist
Brenda DiAntonis

Art Coordinator
Kevin Barnes

Art Director
CJae Froshay

Imaging
Rosa C. See

Product Manager
Phil Garcia

Publisher
Mary D. Smith, M.S. Ed.

Nonfiction Reading Comprehension

Grade 1

Geography

Science

History

Author

Debra J. Housel, M.S. Ed.

Teacher Created Resources

Teacher Created Resources, Inc.
6421 Industry Way
Westminster, CA 92683
www.teachercreated.com

ISBN-0-7439-3381-8

©2002 Teacher Created Resources, Inc.
Reprinted, 2005
Made in U.S.A.

Table of Contents

Introduction 3

How to Use this Book 5

Achievement Graph 7

Practice Passages

   An Odd Fish 8

   Native American Games and Toys 10

Science Passages

   A Whale of a Good Time 12

   Stars 14

   Our Sun and Moon 16

   Plants Are Important 18

   Chewing the Cud 20

   Water 22

Geography Passages

   Air 24

   Don't Catch That Cold! 26

   The Dead Dodos 28

   The Tundra 30

   The Great Lakes 32

   The Desert 34

History Passages

   Becoming Farmers 36

   Don't Play with Fire 38

   The People Who Keep You Safe 40

   The First Clothes 42

   The Fourth of July 44

   The First Thanksgiving 46

Answer Key 48

Introduction

Comprehension is the primary goal of any reading task. Students who comprehend expository text will have more opportunities in life as well as better test performance. Through the use of nonfiction passages followed by exercises that require vital reading and thinking skills, *Nonfiction Reading Comprehension* will help you to develop confident readers and promote the foundation comprehension skills necessary for a lifetime of learning.

Each passage in *Nonfiction Reading Comprehension* covers a grade-level appropriate curriculum topic in geography, history, or science. The activities are time-efficient, allowing students to practice these skills often. To yield the best results, such practice must begin during the second semester or when a solid majority of your class can read independently at primer level.

✤ Essential Comprehension Skills

The questions following each passage in *Nonfiction Reading Comprehension* always appear in the same order and cover seven vital skills:

✧ Locating facts

Questions based on exactly what the text states—who, what, when, where, why, and how many

✧ Identifying sequence

Questions based on chronological order—what happened first, last, and in between

✧ Noting conditions

Questions that ask students to identify similarities and differences, as well as cause-and-effect relationships

✧ Understanding vocabulary in context

Questions based on the ability to infer word meaning from the syntax and semantics of the surrounding text, as well as the ability to recognize known synonyms and antonyms for a newly encountered word

✧ Making inferences

Questions that require students to evaluate, to make decisions, and to draw logical conclusions

✧ Integrating knowledge

Questions that ask readers to draw upon their visualization skills combined with prior knowledge (These questions reinforce the crucial skill of picturing the text.)

✧ Supporting an answer

A short-answer question at the end of each passage to personalize knowledge, state an opinion, and support it

Meeting Standards and Benchmarks

Every passage in *Nonfiction Reading Comprehension* and its comprehension questions cover one or more language arts standards:

Reading	Writing
• Understands how print is organized and read	• Uses frequently used words to express basic ideas
• Uses schema to understand new information presented in text	• Writes complete, simple sentences
• Visualizes what is read in text	• Writes in a logical sequence
• Uses picture and context clues to decode unknown words	• Uses nouns, verbs, adjectives, and pronouns to make writing diverse and interesting
• Self-monitors reading and takes action to increase understanding (self-corrects, rereads if necessary)	• Follows conventions of capitalization, spelling, and punctuation appropriate for grade level
• Makes and revises predictions about text	• States an opinion and supports it in writing
• Integrates new information into personal knowledge base	
• Understands the main idea of simple nonfiction text	
• Reflects on what has been read and develops ideas, opinions, and personal responses	

The specific McREL content area standard and benchmark for each passage appears in a box at the top of each passage. Used with permission from McREL. (Copyright 2000 McREL, Mid-continent Research for Education and Learning. Telephone: 303-337-0990. Website: www.mcrel.org)

✤ Readability

All of the passages have a 0.5–1.9 reading level based on the Flesch-Kincaid Readability Formula. This formula, built into Microsoft Word, determines a readability level by calculating the number of words, syllables, and sentences. Although content area terms can be challenging, students can handle difficult words within the context given. The passages are presented in order of increasing difficulty within each content area.

✤ Preparing Students to Read Nonfiction Text

Prepare your students to read the passages in *Nonfiction Reading Comprehension* by reading aloud each day a short nonfiction selection from another source. Reading expository text aloud is critical to developing your students' ability to read it themselves. Since making predictions is a good way to help students to understand nonfiction, read the beginning of a passage, then stop and ask them to predict what might occur next. Do this at several points throughout your reading of the text.

Talking about nonfiction concepts is also very important. Remember, however, that discussion can never replace reading aloud, because people rarely speak using the vocabulary and complex sentence structures of written language.

How to Use this Book

If you have some students who cannot read the articles independently, allow them to read with a partner, but then have them work through the comprehension questions alone. As soon as possible, move to having all students practice reading and answering the questions independently.

✤ Multiple-Choice Questions

Do the first two passages and related questions (pages 8–11) with the whole class. These passages have the most challenging reading level. Demonstrate your own cognitive process by thinking aloud about how to figure out an answer. This means, essentially, that you tell your students your thoughts as they come to you. Let's say that this is a passage your class has read:

Long ago many grizzly bears lived in America. People were afraid that the bears would disappear. So a law was passed. It was to keep the bears safe from people. It said that people could not hunt the bears. And they could not hurt the bears' homes.

The law worked. Today there are lots more bears. Most of them live in Yellowstone National Park. Sometimes the bears go out of the park. When they do, sometimes they kill cows and sheep. Some people are afraid. They want to shoot any bear that's outside of the park. But others say there are too few bears. They do not want the law changed.

Following the reading, one of the questions is: "In Yellowstone National park, grizzly bears 'a) roam free' or 'b) get caught in traps.'" Tell the students all your thoughts as they occur to you: "Well, let's look back in the article and see what it says about traps." (Refer back to article.) "I don't see anything about traps in the passage. And I did see that there is a law to keep the bears safe. That means they're safe from traps, which are dangerous. So I'm going to select '(a) roam free.' But what if I didn't know what the word 'roam' means? Then I would need to figure out which choice is wrong. The right answer will have to be the other one."

The fourth question is always about vocabulary. Teach students to substitute the word choices for the vocabulary term (bolded) in the passage. For each choice they should ask, "Does this make sense?" This will help them to identify the best choice.

Teach students to look for the key words in a response or question and search for those specific words in the text. Explain that they may need to look for synonyms for the key words. When you go over the practice passages, ask your students to show where they found the correct response in the text.

How to Use this Book (cont.)

✤ Short-Answer Questions

The short-answer question for each passage is an opinion statement with no definitive answer. Each student makes a statement and explains it. While there is no one correct response, it is critical to show them how to support their opinions using facts and logic. Show them a format for response. Have them state their opinions followed by the word "because" and a reason. An example would be "I do not think that whales should be kept at sea parks because they are wild animals. They want to be in the ocean with their friends." Do not award credit unless the student adequately supports his or her conclusion. Before passing back the practice papers, make note of two students with opposing opinions. Then, during the discussion, call on each of these students to read his or her short-answer response to the class. If all your students drew the same conclusion or had the same opinion, come up with support for an opposing one yourself.

For the most effective practice sessions, follow these steps:

- Have students read the text silently and answer the questions.

- Collect all the papers to score them.

- Return the papers to the students and discuss how they determined their answers.

- Point out how students had to use their background knowledge to answer certain questions.

- Call on at least two students with different viewpoints to read and discuss their responses to the short-answer question.

- Have your students complete the achievement bar graph on page 7, showing how many questions they answered correctly for each practice passage. Seeing their scores improve or stay consistently high over time will provide encouragement and motivation.

Scoring the Passages

Since the passages are meant as skill builders, do not include the passage scores in students' class grades. With the students, use the "number correct" approach for scoring the practice passages, especially since this coincides with the student-achievement graph on page 7. However, for your own records and to share with the parents, you may want to keep a track of numeric scores for each student. If you choose to do this, do not write the numeric score on the paper. To generate a numeric score, follow these guidelines:

Multiple-choice questions (6)	15 points each	90 points
Short-answer questions (1)	10 points	10 points
Total		**100 points**

✤ Practice Makes Perfect

The more your students practice, the more competent and confident they will become. Plan to have your class do every exercise in *Nonfiction Reading Comprehension*. If you do so, you will be pleased with your students' improved comprehension of any expository text—within your classroom and beyond its walls.

Achievement Graph

Passage	Number Correct
	1 2 3 4 5 6 7
"An Odd Fish"	
"Native American Games and Toys"	
"A Whale of a Good Time"	
"Stars"	
"Our Sun and Moon"	
"Plants Are Important"	
"Chewing the Cud"	
"Water"	
"Air"	
"Don't Catch That Cold!"	
"The Dead Dodos"	
"The Tundra"	
"The Great Lakes"	
"The Desert"	
"Becoming Farmers"	
"Don't Play with Fire"	
"The People Who Keep You Safe"	
"The First Clothes"	
"The Fourth of July"	
"The First Thanksgiving"	

Science Standard: Understands how species depend on one another and on the environment for survival

Benchmark: Knows that living things are found almost everywhere in the world and that distinct environments support the life of different types of plants and animals

An Odd Fish

A seahorse does not swim like other fish do. It moves through the water like a rocking horse. Its head looks like a horse's head. It uses its long **snout** to suck up food.

The seahorse has a hard body that feels like bones. It can wrap its tail around a piece of seaweed. It hides there so that sea turtles and sharks do not find it.

A male seahorse gives birth to the babies! The female puts her eggs into his pouch. He carries the eggs for six weeks. Then the little babies pop out and swim away.

An Odd Fish

Comprehension Questions

Fill in the bubble next to the right answer.

1. A seahorse's head looks like

ⓐ a horse's.

ⓑ seaweed.

2. What happens last?

ⓐ The male carries the eggs.

ⓑ The babies swim away.

3. What makes a seahorse different from other fish?

ⓐ It swims in a different way.

ⓑ It is a horse, not a fish.

4. A snout is

ⓐ an ear.

ⓑ a nose and mouth.

5. Why does the seahorse hide from sea turtles and sharks?

ⓐ They want to eat the seahorse.

ⓑ They are playing hide and seek.

6. Picture a seahorse. What is it doing?

ⓐ It has its tail wrapped around seaweed.

ⓑ It is jumping out of the water.

7. Would you like to see a seahorse? Why?

_____

- -

_____

_____

- -

_____

History Standard: Understands the folklore and other cultural contributions from various regions of the United States and how they helped to form a national heritage

Benchmark: Knows the differences between toys and games children played long ago and the toys and games of today

Native American Games and Toys

Have you ever played cat's cradle? That string game comes from Native Americans. Have you ever seen a lacrosse game? The players catch and throw a ball with nets on poles. That was a Native American game, too.

Native American boys and girls played other games as well. They hid a small rock in a shoe and took turns guessing which shoe it was in. They made marks on flat stones. They used them as dice in **games of chance**.

The children played with toys. Little girls had dolls made of corncobs. Small boys had bows and arrows. They shot at logs. Older boys shot at moving hoops.

Native-American Games and Toys

Comprehension Questions

Fill in the bubble next to the right answer.

1. What were the Native American girls' dolls made with?

ⓐ flat stones

ⓑ corncobs

2. What happened first?

ⓐ There are lacrosse teams in many schools.

ⓑ Native Americans played lacrosse.

3. How are today's toys different from the Native American toys?

ⓐ No one plays with dolls or bows and arrows anymore.

ⓑ Their toys were made of things found outside.

4. Games of chance are

ⓐ games you win by luck.

ⓑ games you win by skill.

5. Why did boys use bows and arrows?

ⓐ because they didn't like the other games

ⓑ because when they grew up, it would help them to hunt

6. Picture Native American children long ago. What are they doing?

ⓐ playing with stones and sticks

ⓑ pulling a wagon with toys in it

7. What game or toy do you like the best? Why?

_____

_____

_____

_____

Science Standard: Understands how species depend on one another and on the environment for survival

Benchmark: Knows that living things are found almost everywhere in the world and that distinct environments support the life of different types of plants and animals

A Whale of a Good Time

Dolphins are little whales. But most whales are big. The blue whale is the **largest** animal on Earth.

Whales live in the sea. They swim in groups. They make sounds to "talk." All whales have a hole on top of their heads. They do not stay under the water all of the time. They need to come up for air. When they go back under the water, the hole shuts.

Whales are mammals, just like us. They are smart. They can learn tricks. You may see a dolphin at a sea park. They are fun to watch!

A Whale of a Good Time

Comprehension Questions

Fill in the bubble next to the right answer.

1. Most whales are

ⓐ big.

ⓑ small.

2. What happens first?

ⓐ The whale does a trick.

ⓑ The man teaches the whale a trick.

3. How is a whale different from a fish?

ⓐ All fish live in fresh water.

ⓑ A fish is not a mammal.

4. What word means the same as *largest*?

ⓐ biggest

ⓑ weakest

5. What trick might a sea park whale do?

ⓐ jump through a hoop

ⓑ sing a song

6. Picture a whale jumping out of the water. When it comes down, you see a big

ⓐ fog.

ⓑ splash.

7. Do you think that whales like to live in sea parks? Why?

_____

_____

_____

Science Standard: Understands essential ideas about the composition and structure of the universe and the Earth's place in it

Benchmark: Knows that the stars are innumerable, unevenly dispersed, and of unequal brightness

Stars

When you look up in the sky at night, what do you see? If it is a clear night, you will see stars. Stars are all of the little lights you see in the sky. There are many, many stars. There are so many that no one can count them all!

Stars are not all the same. Some are big. Some are small. Some give more light than others do. The sun is a star. It isn't the biggest one. But it is **closer** to our Earth than the others. That's why we see it so well.

Stars

Comprehension Questions

Fill in the bubble next to the right answer.

1. In the night sky there are many

(a) moons.

(b) stars.

2. What happens first?

(a) You see the stars in the sky.

(b) The sun goes down.

3. What does the sun send to Earth?

(a) light

(b) storms

4. *Closer* means

(a) nearer.

(b) bigger.

5. What makes stars different from each other?

(a) They are not all the same size.

(b) They are made up of different things.

6. Picture a night when you can see many stars. What is *not* is the sky?

(a) the moon

(b) thick clouds

7. Would you like to learn more about stars? Why?

_____

- -

_____

_____

- -

_____

Science Standard: Understands energy types, sources, and conversions, and their relationship to heat and temperature

Benchmark: Knows that the sun supplies heat and light to Earth

Our Sun and Moon

The sun is a big star. It gives heat and light to Earth. The sun is always shining. During our night, it shines on the other side of the world. The sun is there on cloudy days. The clouds hide it.

The moon has no light of its own. It **reflects** the sun's light. The moon seems to change shape. But it does not. The whole moon is still there. We just see less of it when part of the moon is in the Earth's shadow.

Our Sun and Moon

Comprehension Questions

Fill in the bubble next to the right answer.

1. Which looks like it changes shape?

ⓐ the sun

ⓑ the moon

2. What happens at the start of our day?

ⓐ The sun comes up.

ⓑ The sun goes down.

3. What would the Earth be like without the sun?

ⓐ It would be hot and bright.

ⓑ It would be cold and dark.

4. *Reflects* means

ⓐ drinks.

ⓑ shows.

5. What happens when the moon is completely in the Earth's shadow?

ⓐ We can not see the moon at all.

ⓑ We have a full, round moon.

6. Picture a very cloudy day. Which is true?

ⓐ You see the sun shine in a blue sky.

ⓑ You do not see the sun at all. Clouds block some of its light.

7. Would you like to visit the moon? Why?

_____

- -

_____
_____

- -

_____

Science Standard: Knows the general structure and functions of cells in organisms

Benchmark: Knows that animals require air, water, food, and shelter; plants require air, water, nutrients, and light

Plants Are Important

All plants need water, air, and light. Plants do not eat. They use the light from the sun to make their own food. That is why a plant always grows towards the sun. Plants make the food in their leaves. Then they store the food in their stems and roots. They use this food on **gloomy** days when the sun does not shine.

If there were no plants, there would be no life on Earth. Plants start every food chain. An animal eats the plant. Or it eats the seeds or fruit of the plant. Then another animal eats that animal. Some animals eat both plants and animals.

Plants are Important

Comprehension Questions

Fill in the bubble next to the right answer.

1. Plants can not

ⓐ eat food.

ⓑ use food.

2. What happens first?

ⓐ A plant uses food from its roots.

ⓑ A plant makes food from the sun.

3. Where do plants get water?

ⓐ the ground

ⓑ the store

4. *Gloomy* means

ⓐ dark.

ⓑ bright.

5. How do plants keep living things alive?

ⓐ All animals eat plants.

ⓑ Every animal eats plants or animals that eat plants.

6. Picture a bush growing in the shade of a tree. How does it look?

ⓐ Most of the bush's branches are growing towards the shade.

ⓑ Most of the bush's branches are growing away from the shade.

7. What plant do you like best? Why?

_____

- -

_____

_____

- -

_____

Science Standard: Understands the cycling of matter and flow of energy through the living environment

Benchmark: Knows that plants and animals need certain resources for energy and growth (e.g., food, water, light and air)

Chewing the Cud

A deer is afraid when it is in an open field. It thinks that other animals might attack it. So it tears off big pieces of leaves and branches from bushes. But it does not chew them. It **swallows** them whole!

This food gets stored in a special part of the deer's stomach. When the deer is back in the woods, it feels safer. Then it brings up the stored food, or cud. The deer chews the cud. Chewing the cud breaks the food into little pieces. Then the deer's body can use it.

Chewing the Cud

Comprehension Questions

Fill in the bubble next to the right answer.

1. What is in cud?

ⓐ leaves and bark

ⓑ meat

2. What happens last?

ⓐ The deer grabs branches and leaves from a field.

ⓑ The deer chews the cud.

3. Why does the deer chew cud?

ⓐ to break its food into small pieces its body can use

ⓑ to keep its teeth from getting too long

4. *Swallows* means

ⓐ smells.

ⓑ gulps.

5. Which animal would a deer be afraid of?

ⓐ a wolf

ⓑ a rabbit

6. Picture a deer getting food. Where is it eating?

ⓐ from the top branches of a big tree

ⓑ from the bottom branches of a little tree

7. Do you like deer? Why?

_____

- -

_____

_____

- -

_____

Science Standard: Knows the general structure and functions of cells in organisms

Benchmark: Knows that animals require air, water, food and shelter; plants require air, water, nutrients, and light

Water

You know that there is more water than land on Earth. But did you know that there are two kinds of water? There is fresh water. And there is salt water. There is lots more salt water than fresh water on Earth. Salt water is in the sea. We cannot drink it. It would make us ill. But most sea animals must stay in salt water. If they are put in fresh water, they die.

Lakes and rivers hold fresh water. Rain, snow, and ice are **forms** of fresh water. Many animals and all plants and people need fresh water. Without water there could be no life on Earth.

Water

Comprehension Questions

Fill in the bubble next to the right answer.

1. What kind of water can people drink?

ⓐ salt water

ⓑ fresh water

2. What happens last?

ⓐ A person gets sick.

ⓑ A person drinks salt water.

3. Why do fresh water animals have to stay in fresh water?

ⓐ because salt water is different and not good for them

ⓑ because there isn't enough salt water for them

4. The word *forms* means

ⓐ kinds.

ⓑ spots.

5. What happens when snow melts?

ⓐ It turns into salt water.

ⓑ It turns into fresh water.

6. Picture a waterfall. What kind of water is it?

ⓐ fresh water

ⓑ salt water

7. Which do you like best: rain, ice, or snow? Why?

_____

_____

_____

_____

Geography Standard: Understands how human actions modify the physical environment

Benchmark: Knows ways in which people depend on the physical environment

Air

Air is all around us. We cannot see it. But it takes up space. It takes up space inside of a balloon. When the balloon pops, the air **rushes** out.

When air moves outside, we call it wind. Warm air goes up. Cold air goes down. Wind, warm air, and cold air make our weather change.

We must take care to keep our air clean. We need to breathe air. All plants and animals do. Even fish breathe air. Their gills take air out of the water.

Air

Comprehension Questions

Fill in the bubble next to the right answer.

1. What needs air?

ⓐ just animals

ⓑ both plants and animals

2. What happens last?

ⓐ The balloon hits something sharp.

ⓑ The air goes out of the balloon.

3. When the wind blows,

ⓐ warm and cold air move around outdoors.

ⓑ no rain can fall.

4. *Rushes* means

ⓐ moves slowly.

ⓑ moves quickly.

5. Why do we need clean air?

ⓐ If we breathe dirty air, it may make us sick.

ⓑ Clean air costs less than dirty air.

6. Picture a person smoking in a room. What do you see?

ⓐ The air in the room is clean.

ⓑ The air in the room is full of smoke.

7. Do you like windy days? Why?

_____

- -

_____

_____

- -

_____

Geography Standard: Understands the changes that occur in the meaning, use, distribution, and importance of resources

Benchmark: Understands the role that resources play in our daily lives (medicine)

Don't Catch that Cold!

You have probably had a cold. You coughed. Your nose ran. Your head hurt. You felt bad! The cold came from a **virus**. A virus is not alive. But if it gets into your body, it makes you sick.

If the germs can't get inside you, they can't make you sick. Most germs get in through your mouth and nose. So always wash your hands before eating.

You will get over a cold in about a week. But some germs can kill you. That is why you get shots. They keep you safe from really bad viruses.

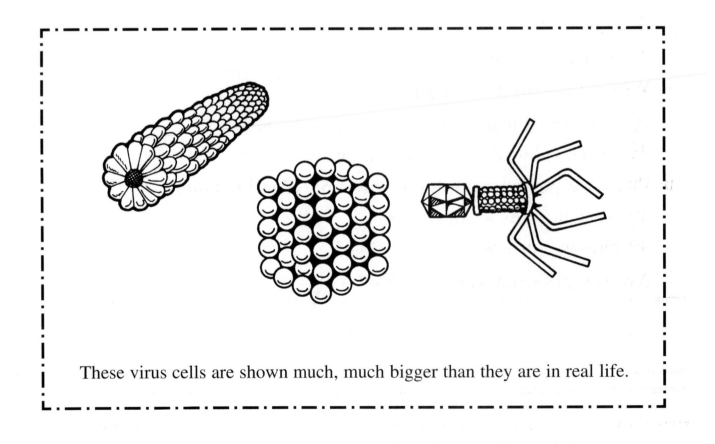

These virus cells are shown much, much bigger than they are in real life.

Don't Catch that Cold!

Comprehension Questions

Fill in the bubble next to the right answer.

1. How soon will you get over a cold?

ⓐ about one year

ⓑ about one week

2. What happened first?

ⓐ A cold germ got into your body.

ⓑ You got sick with a cold.

3. After a virus gets into your body, it

ⓐ keeps you safe.

ⓑ makes you feel bad.

4. A *virus* is

ⓐ a germ.

ⓑ a shot.

5. Why do nurses give shots?

ⓐ to make children cry

ⓑ to keep children safe from germs

6. Picture a boy who has a bad cold. What is he doing?

ⓐ scratching all over

ⓑ blowing his nose

7. Are you glad that there are shots? Why?

_____

- -

_____

_____

- -

_____

Geography Standard: Understands how geography is used to interpret the past

Benchmark: Knows how areas of a community have changed over time (in terms of changes in plant and animal population, etc.)

The Dead Dodos

Dodo birds had only one home. They lived on an island in the Indian Ocean. When **sailors** found their island, the birds were in big trouble. These birds could not fly. They were easy to catch. So the men ate them.

Pigs came on the ships. Sometimes the men could not catch them. Then the pigs stayed on the island. The pigs ate all of the dodo birds' eggs.

In 1680 the last dodo bird died. There are none of these birds left on Earth.

The Dead Dodos

Comprehension Questions

Fill in the bubble next to the right answer.

1. Which animal died out?

ⓐ dodo birds

ⓑ pigs

2. What happened last?

ⓐ Sailors found the island.

ⓑ Pigs were loose on the island.

3. What made the dodo birds easy to catch?

ⓐ They could not fly.

ⓑ They could not run.

4. *Sailors* are

ⓐ the people who keep animals safe.

ⓑ the people who work on ships.

5. Will there ever again be dodo birds on Earth?

ⓐ yes, someday soon

ⓑ no, never

6. Picture a dodo bird's nest from long ago. Where is it?

ⓐ on the ground

ⓑ high up in a tree

7. Do you think that the sailors did something wrong? Explain. _____

_____

_____

 **Geography Standard:** Understands the physical and human characteristics of place

Benchmark: Knows that places can be defined in terms of their predominant human and physical characteristics

The Tundra

The tundra is a flat land in the far north. The tundra is cold and windy. There is little rain. The summer is very short.

No trees live there. Their roots can not grow. The dirt under the ground is always **frozen**. Only small plants live on the tundra.

Many animals there have white fur in the winter. They have brown fur in the summer. The color change helps them to blend in with snow in the winter and dirt in the summer. It makes it harder for other animals to see them. This helps them to stay safe.

The Tundra

Comprehension Questions

Fill in the bubble next to the right answer.

1. What does not grow on the tundra?

ⓐ any plants

ⓑ any trees

2. What happens last?

ⓐ It turns to winter on the tundra.

ⓑ The animals' hair turns white.

3. Why do tundra animals have fur color changes?

ⓐ to help them hide from other animals

ⓑ to make it easy for other animals to find them

4. *Frozen* means

ⓐ cold and hard.

ⓑ warm and soft.

5. Why do plants have a hard time growing on the tundra?

ⓐ Their roots can not get down into the frozen dirt.

ⓑ They do not get enough sun.

6. Picture a rabbit living on the tundra in summer. What color is its fur?

ⓐ white

ⓑ brown

7. Would you like to live on the tundra? Why?

_____

- -

_____

_____

- -

_____

Geography Standard: Understands the concept of regions

Benchmark: Knows areas that can be classified as regions according to physical criteria and human criteria

The Great Lakes

The five Great Lakes are very big. They can be seen from space! The lakes hold a lot of fresh water. One is Lake Superior. It is the second biggest lake in the world.

The lakes are between America and Canada. On one side of four lakes is America. On the other side is Canada. But this is not true for one lake. Lake Michigan is inside the U.S.

The Great Lakes are **linked**. A ship can move from one to the other. Many ships go from lake to lake. They bring things to people. These ships may even go out to the sea. Then they can go to other countries.

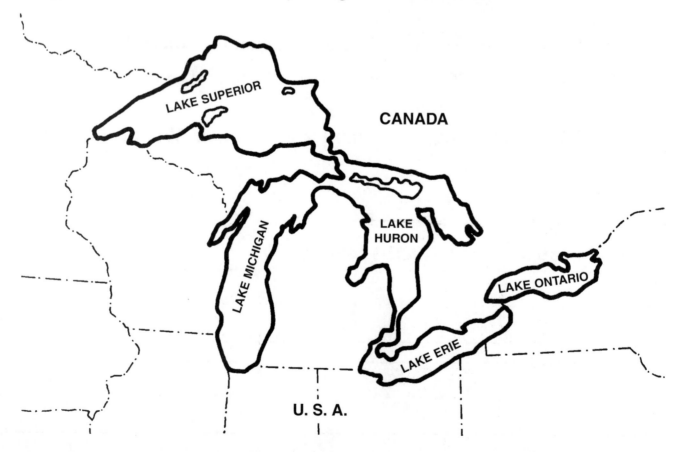

The Great Lakes

Comprehension Questions

Fill in the bubble next to the right answer.

1. What is the second biggest lake in the world?

   ⓐ Lake Erie

   ⓑ Lake Superior

2. What two countries share the Great Lakes?

   ⓐ America and Canada

   ⓑ America and Mexico

3. Can a ship from the sea reach the Great Lakes?

   ⓐ no

   ⓑ yes

4. *Linked* means

   ⓐ stacked.

   ⓑ joined.

5. Look at the map. How could a ship in Lake Ontario reach Lake Huron?

   ⓐ It would cross Lake Erie.

   ⓑ It would cross Lake Superior.

6. Picture a ship bringing things to people in the Great Lakes. What is the ship made of?

   ⓐ wood

   ⓑ metal

7. Would you like to go on a boat ride through all five Great Lakes? Why?

_____

_____

_____

_____

Geography Standard: Understands the physical and human characteristics of place

Benchmark: Knows that places can be defined in terms of their predominant human and physical characteristics

The Desert

A desert is hot and dry. Very little rain falls. Wind blows the sand. This forms dunes. Each day the sun heats up the desert. Then at night the desert gets very cold!

Many kinds of animals and plants live in a desert. Most animals sleep in the day. They come out at night to hunt. Some animals, like the camel, store water in their bodies. They can go for weeks without a drink. Cactus plants store water, too. Their sharp **needles** keep the animals from taking it.

Few people live in the desert. They need more water than they can find

The Desert

Comprehension Questions

Fill in the bubble next to the right answer.

1. What kind of plant can store water?

ⓐ a cactus

ⓑ grass

2. Is the desert hot at all times?

ⓐ no

ⓑ yes

3. Why do some plants and animals store water?

ⓐ because it snows in the desert

ⓑ because it is dry in the desert

4. *Needles* on a plant are

ⓐ pointed things.

ⓑ purple flowers.

5. Why are most desert animals awake at night?

ⓐ They can not see during the day.

ⓑ It is cool enough to come out then.

6. Picture a desert during the day. What do you see?

ⓐ lots of animals

ⓑ lots of sand

7. Would you like to visit a desert? Why? _____

_____

_____

_____

History Standard: Understands major discoveries in science and technology, some of their social and economic effects, and the major scientists and inventors responsible for them

Benchmark: Understands the differences between hunters and gatherers and people who cultivated plants and raised domesticated animals for food

Becoming Farmers

Long, long ago people did not know how to grow food. So they looked for fruits and nuts. They hunted and ate animals. The animals moved around. So the people had to move around, too. At night they looked for a cave to stay in. When they couldn't find one, they often got cold and wet.

Then people found out that if they put seeds in the ground, plants would grow. Then they could eat the plants or their seeds. This let the people stay in one place. They made homes and grew **crops**. They stored up food, too. They lived longer.

Becoming Farmers

Comprehension Questions

Fill in the bubble next to the right answer.

1. After people became farmers they

ⓐ had a longer life than when they moved with the animals.

ⓑ had a shorter life than when they moved with the animals.

2. What happened first?

ⓐ People stayed in one place.

ⓑ People went where the animals went.

3. Why did people follow the animals?

ⓐ They needed to eat the animals for food.

ⓑ They felt bored.

4. *Crops* are

ⓐ plants that have flowers.

ⓑ plants that people use for food.

5. What was a good thing about learning to farm?

ⓐ The people could save food.

ⓑ The people stopped eating animals.

6. Picture the people inside the caves. What gives them light?

ⓐ a flashlight

ⓑ a fire

7. Which would you rather do: follow animals or grow food? Why?

- -

- -

History Standard: Understands how democratic values came to be, and how they have been exemplified by people, events, and symbols

Benchmark: Knows how different groups of people in the community have taken responsibility for the common good (firefighters, doctors)

Don't Play with Fire

Be careful near fire. Clothes and paper burn easily. Keep away from hot stoves and grills. Never play with matches or a lighter.

If you ever catch on fire, do not run! Drop to the ground. Roll around until the fire goes out. Then get help. Burns are bad. You must see a doctor right away.

Have a smoke **alarm** in your home. If you hear it, get out! Fire can move fast. Smoke can, too. Smoke rises. So stay low. Try not to breathe smoke. If you cannot reach a door, go out a window.

Stay back. Firefighters will put out the fire.

Don't Play with Fire

Comprehension Questions

Fill in the bubble next to the right answer.

1. What catches fire easily?

ⓐ green grass

ⓑ paper

2. If you hear a smoke alarm, what should you do first?

ⓐ Call the firefighters.

ⓑ Get out of the house.

3. Why do you need to see a doctor if you get a burn?

ⓐ because you can not treat a bad burn yourself

ⓑ because you need a bandage

4. The word *alarm* means

ⓐ a noise that warns.

ⓑ the sound of a horn.

5. Why shouldn't you run if you catch on fire?

ⓐ Running is too hard to do.

ⓑ Running would not put out the fire.

6. Picture a house on fire. What is coming out of its windows?

ⓐ smoke

ⓑ bugs

7. Do you think it's good that your school has fire drills? Why?

_____

- -

_____

- -

_____

History Standard: Understands how democratic values came to be, and how they have been exemplified by people, events, and symbols

Benchmark: Knows how different groups of people in the community have taken responsibility for the common good (doctors, police, firefighters, ambulance workers)

The People Who Keep You Safe

Many people work to keep you safe. Your doctor wants to keep you well. When you are sick, your doctor gives you pills so you will get better.

The police make sure that no one breaks into your home. They keep watch so that no one hurts you.

Firefighters put out fires. If your home catches on fire, they come. They spray water from hoses. The fire will go out. Your home may be saved.

Ambulance workers hurry to you if you are hurt badly. They take care of you. They rush you to the **hospital**. They can save your life.

The People Who Keep You Safe

Comprehension Questions

Fill in the bubble next to the right answer.

1. What do ambulance workers do?

ⓐ They take hurt or very sick people to a hospital.

ⓑ They use hoses to fight fires.

2. What happens last?

ⓐ A person calls the ambulance.

ⓑ The hurt child goes away in the ambulance.

3. Is a firefighter always safe when fighting a fire?

ⓐ no

ⓑ yes

4. A *hospital* is

ⓐ where the firefighters work.

ⓑ where doctors help people who are hurt.

5. Who do you call if someone broke into your home?

ⓐ the police

ⓑ the doctor

6. Picture a doctor's office. Who else works there?

ⓐ nurses

ⓑ police

7. What would you like to be when you grow up? Why?

_____

- -

_____

_____

- -

_____

History Standard: Understands the historical perspective

Benchmark: Understands that specific ideas had an impact on history

The First Clothes

Long, long ago people had no clothes. They lived in warm places. They did not need clothes. But the people followed animals. So over time they moved to colder places. They did not like the cold. So after they killed an animal they put its skin around them. It was like a **blanket**. Then they felt warmer.

Over time they learned to make needles from bird bones. They made thread from strong grass. They cut the animal skins with sharp rocks or bones. Then they sewed the pieces together into the first clothes. The clothes kept the people warm.

The First Clothes

Comprehension Questions

Fill in the bubble next to the right answer.

1. What did the early people use for needles?

ⓐ bird bones

ⓑ strong grasses

2. What happened first?

ⓐ People used animal skins to stay warm.

ⓑ People did not wear clothes.

3. Why did the people want to stay warm?

ⓐ It didn't feel good to be cold and they could get sick.

ⓑ They wanted to look good.

4. A *blanket* is

ⓐ clothes.

ⓑ something we cover up with.

5. Why did the people make animal skins into clothes?

ⓐ They did not know what else to do with the animal skins.

ⓑ The clothes stayed on better than the animal skin blanket did.

6. Picture a person wearing some of the first clothes. What do you see on the clothes?

ⓐ fur

ⓑ buttons

7. What piece of clothing do you like to wear the most? Why?

_____

_____

_____

_____

History Standard: Understands how democratic values came to be, and how they have been exemplified by people, events, and symbols

Benchmark: Understands the reasons that Americans celebrate national holidays

The Fourth of July

We see fireworks on the Fourth of July. There are **parades**. Most people have the day off. Why? It is America's birthday.

At one time a king ruled America. He lived across the sea. The people did not like this. They wanted to make their own laws. They wanted to be free. So they told the king. It was July 4, 1776.

The king got mad. He sent men to fight. When the war was over, America was free.

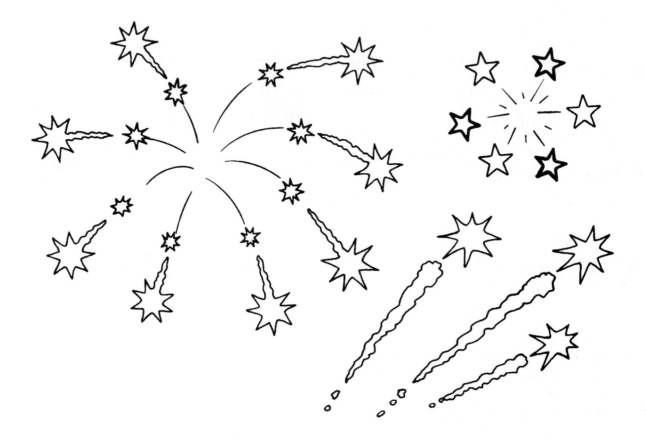

The Fourth of July

Comprehension Questions

Fill in the bubble next to the right answer.

1. On July 4, 1776,

    ⓐ a king started to rule America.

    ⓑ the people told the king that they were free.

2. What happened first?

    ⓐ The people had parades and fireworks on July 4th.

    ⓑ The people fought to be free.

3. America's birthday is July 4th because

    ⓐ that is the day that the king lost the war.

    ⓑ that is the day that the people said they were free.

4. During *parades*

    ⓐ bands play music.

    ⓑ people run.

5. What would have happened if America lost the fight?

    ⓐ The people would have made their own laws.

    ⓑ The king would have stayed the ruler.

6. Picture the king on July 4, 1776. What is the look on his face?

    ⓐ mad

    ⓑ happy

7. What is the best part of the 4th of July? Why?

_____

_____

_____

_____

_____

History Standard: Understands how democratic values came to be, and how they have been exemplified by people, events, and symbols

Benchmark: Understands the reasons that Americans celebrate certain national holidays

The First Thanksgiving

In 1620 the Pilgrims left England. They wanted their own land. They sailed in a ship called the *Mayflower*. When they reached America, they named their new home Plymouth.

The first winter was hard. There wasn't much to eat. Half of the people died. In the spring, Native Americans found them. They gave the Pilgrims corn seeds. They told them where to fish and dig for clams.

By that fall the people had lots of food. They had a big **feast**. They asked the Native Americans to come. They ate for three days! It was the first Thanksgiving.

The First Thanksgiving

Comprehension Questions

Fill in the bubble next to the right answer.

1. What was the name of the ship the Pilgrims sailed on?

ⓐ *Plymouth*

ⓑ *Mayflower*

2. What happened last?

ⓐ The people almost starved to death.

ⓑ The people met the Native Americans.

3. Did it help the Pilgrims when the Native Americans gave them corn seeds?

ⓐ Yes, because then the Pilgrims had a crop of corn.

ⓑ No, because the Pilgrims didn't know what to do with them.

4. The word *feast* means

ⓐ meal.

ⓑ wedding.

5. Why did the Pilgrims ask the Native Americans to come?

ⓐ because the Native Americans had given them help

ⓑ because they wanted to stop the war with the Native Americans

6. Picture the first Thanksgiving. What food do you see?

ⓐ oranges

ⓑ pies

7. Do you enjoy Thanksgiving Day? Why?

_____

_____

_____

_____

Answer Key

Page 9
1. a
2. b
3. a
4. b
5. a
6. a
7. Accept well-supported answers.

Page 11
1. b
2. b
3. b
4. a
5. b
6. a
7. Accept well-supported answers.

Page 13
1. a
2. a
3. b
4. a
5. a
6. b
7. Accept well-supported answers.

Page 15
1. b
2. b
3. a
4. a
5. a
6. b
7. Accept well-supported answers.

Page 17
1. b
2. a
3. b
4. b
5. a
6. b
7. Accept well-supported answers.

Page 19
1. a
2. b
3. a
4. a
5. b
6. b
7. Accept well-supported answers.

Page 21
1. a
2. b
3. a
4. b
5. a
6. b
7. Accept well-supported answers.

Page 23
1. b
2. a
3. a
4. a
5. b
6. a
7. Accept well-supported answers.

Page 25
1. b
2. b
3. a
4. b
5. a
6. b
7. Accept well-supported answers.

Page 27
1. b
2. a
3. b
4. a
5. b
6. b
7. Accept well-supported answers.

Page 29
1. a
2. b
3. a
4. b
5. b
6. a
7. Accept well-supported answers.

Page 31
1. b
2. b
3. a
4. a
5. a
6. b
7. Accept well-supported answers.

Page 33
1. b
2. a
3. b
4. b
5. a
6. b
7. Accept well-supported answers.

Page 35
1. a
2. a
3. b
4. a
5. b
6. b
7. Accept well-supported answers.

Page 37
1. a
2. b
3. a
4. b
5. a
6. b
7. Accept well-supported answers.

Page 39
1. b
2. b
3. a
4. a
5. b
6. a
7. Accept well-supported answers.

Page 41
1. a
2. b
3. a
4. b
5. a
6. a
7. Accept well-supported answers.

Page 43
1. a
2. b
3. a
4. b
5. b
6. a
7. Accept well-supported answers.

Page 45
1. b
2. b
3. b
4. a
5. b
6. a
7. Accept well-supported answers.

Page 47
1. b
2. b
3. a
4. a
5. a
6. b
7. Accept well-supported answers.

Teacher Created Resources

"Created by Teachers for Teachers"

Quality Resource Books

- language arts
- social studies
- math
- science
- technology
- the arts

Decorative Products

- 2-sided decorations
- 3-D decorations
- accent dazzlers
- awards
- badges
- banners
- bookmarks
- border trim
- bulletin boards
- file folders
- incentive charts
- name plates
- name tags
- notepads
- pocket folders
- postcards
- stickers

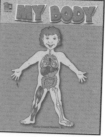

For more information, visit our Web site: www.teachercreated.com

AR73 10/04

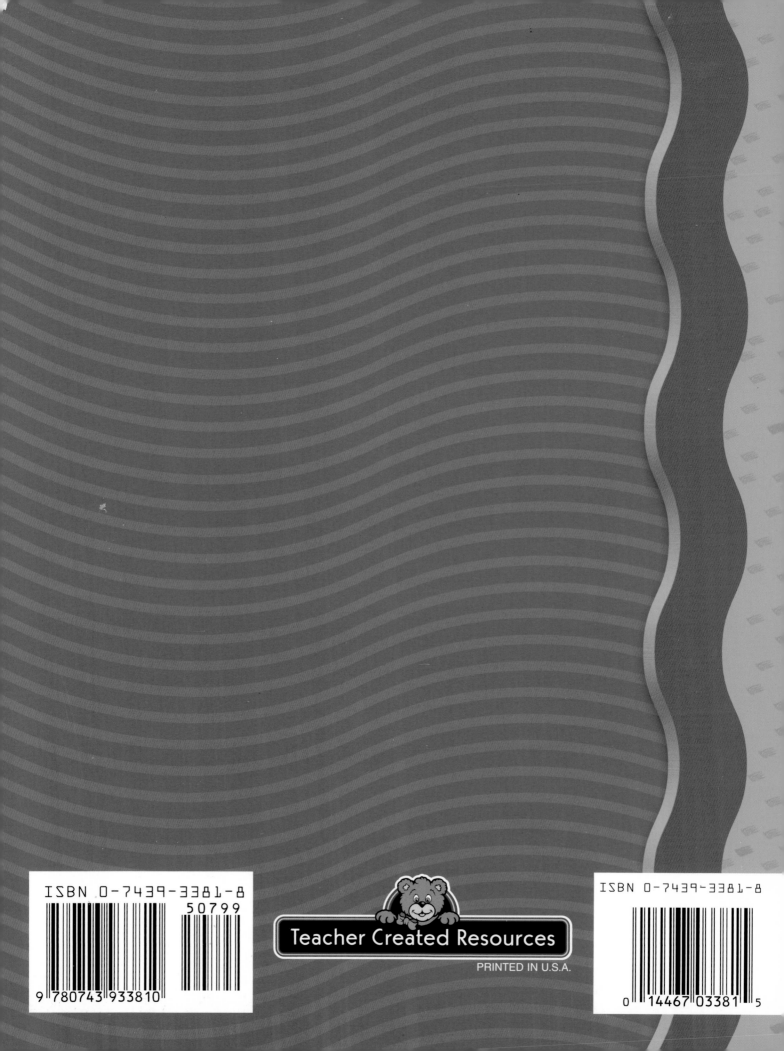

ISBN 0-7439-3381-8

50799

Teacher Created Resources

PRINTED IN U.S.A.

9 780743 933810

ISBN 0-7439-3381-8

0 14467 03381 5